{ colour of morning

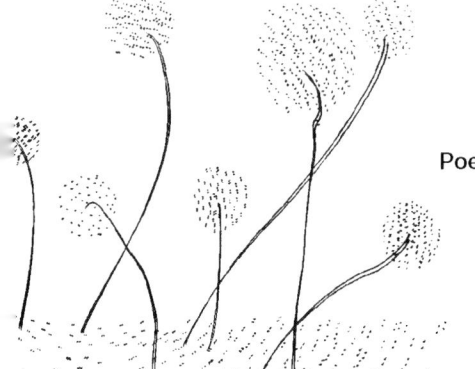

Poems ~ Steve Cutmore

Sketches ~ Martin Lloyd

For my sister Julia

Poems ~ Steve Cutmore
Sketches ~ Martin Lloyd
Original Design ~ Alex Valy
Additional editing & design ~ James & Frances Stretton,
Author Photograph ~ Sean Halligan
Cover & Inside Photographs ~ Fran H Mulliner

Guidance ~ Margaret & John Crompton
Kindly Financed ~ F & E

A Jazz Republic Publication © 2007
e-mail: jazzrepublic@hotmail.com

All rights reserved © Steve Cutmore 2007
The author asserts the moral right to be identified as the author of this work

A catalogue record for this book is available from the British Library

Printed & Bound in England by Parchments of Oxford

ISBN   978-0-9555280-0-2

e-mail: info@stevecutmore.com
web: www.stevecutmore.com

Contents

Blood brothers 8

Manslaughtered 10

Letter to a friend 12

Mister mentor 16

Once upon a time 19

The view from the window 20

A lonely messiah 22

My urban lover 24

Walk talk eat 26

Ten rows back 28

Theodore & Grace 31

Bastards 32

Father figure 34

Box 40

Blood brothers

For eight years
We have sucked the throbbing hearts from strawberries
Drained bottles of their bloodwine
Raced together in bumper cars like children while the wind blew our hair back
We were INVINCIBLE
like crazy gunslingers in an Italian movie
and music music
Music was our lives is our lives
You remember
Playing till the last cash registers stopped ringing
but still singing none the less

For eight years
We have stood next to angels
Questioned the very divide of time
Smiling on life with a warmth that would shame the deepest gold
buried here on this lonely planet
We have sat in the arms of oaks
Watching just watching the hubbub of it all
And fighting Fighting with ourselves

Fighting with each other but fighting
with ourselves
proved to be the bloodiest

Yes for eight years
They could never say that we hadn't
touched the very essence of it
that we never searched our very souls
Into every corner of those unlit rooms
Stalking the corridors like pearl thieves
Stumbling upon truths upon untruths
Hiding beneath the pebbles where the
starfish live

We have come this far
We have come this far and further
And no one could say we hadn't
No one could say we hadn't
Loved could they

manslaughtered

I am weak
bruised swollen
wretched
bludgeoned beaten
sodden sopping scared
useless
respite – there is none
skull sucked searched
blades blunt
blades blunt bleeding
thirst me...
there is nowhere to run
trapped snared
bitten
ravaged raped rabid
gagged
whining whimpering wasted
wanton
want me...
smashed spikes split hands and feet
as eros utters his plaintive cry
heal me...
starving gaunt crushed
frenzied tourniquet tugging

stomach pump pumping ripped
swallow me...
bones burnt broken
used
gawking bulging bulking
barking gnawing
gored
touch me...
there is nothing left
nothing
barren desolation
broken
broken by voice
voice hoarse
voice hoarse from
screaming
screaming
I
Love
You

Letter to a friend

Green iron sandwich
gun metal blue
Fresh flower silence
soft squeaky shoes
Now Saturday's come
I knew it would happen on a Saturday
They're going to wire your head
I mean *my* head
They're trying to put me right
they think they've got the answers
but I told them I was dead dead dead

Round and round the mulberry bush
there's a buckle on my shoe
and poetry what's that
White funk on Black history
some smart arse comment on Yorkshire
A parasite that sucks on someone else's grief
a Chagall for all seasons

A stale rubber bit
clenched between my teeth
And all because
No not because the lady loves fucking Milk Tray

But because they thought
they thought I had a fit
So they wired up my head
'cause they thought they'd put me right
They think they've got the answers
but I told them I was dead dead dead

I'm in a green iron sandwich
that's gun metal blue
My blue smoke suicide
I'm in love with you nurse *nurse me*

And the man from Del Monte
He hides behind the screen
washing his hands slowly slowly
Bureaucratically clean

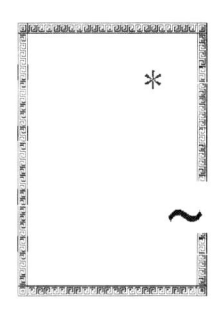

{ ....

...}

Mister mentor

for Billaal

Hey sax man
down on the street
under the neon
I seen you there many times
tappin your feet
making that melody so very sweet

Hey mister man
Play me songs
Play me a tune
that's what they say
Give me somethin cool
Play me somethin hot
Give me somethin dirty
Give me somethin
right now give me some rock

What the hell you doin man
what is that stuff
I said get on the beat
Come on playboy dance for me
Tap for me
Stand on your mother head for me

But they cant hear what you hear
they aint singin the same song
they see the sax man with a crook
in his neck
down on the street
lots of pretty pretty women
dancin under the neon
pushin silver from their hands
while you keep jabbin the beat

There he is again
that dude with crazy jazz in his head
Said hey man gimme that thing
Let me blow
Let me go
Let me mojo
Then I'll pay
See here
You earn the right to play on my street
You hear me
You gotta earn the right to play on my street
You give em a bottom 'B'
I think they understand

Hey mister man
yer fingers cold yet
yer heart beatin fast
yer lungs poppin yet
Yeah I hear you cry
I see you ask
is this OK
Hey you smile for me
tell me this is alright
tell me tonight
tell me around midnight

Said hey mister sax man
I'll play for you tonight
I'll play you a melody real sweet
Yeah I'll play for you tonight
down on the street

Lets play some Bird
Lets play some Young
Lets play some Getz
Lets play some Dex
Lets play any damn thing
Come on
Lets go subtone trillin
Manic octave leapin
Lets mash up the modes
Lets rip-rag the notes
Lets rough up the beat
Lets scream up high
Lets kick up a din
Lets bawl at the sky

Yeah you mister sax man
You and me
under the neon
down on blue street

Lets bebop to the rhythm
Lets swing off the beat
Lets blow hard
Lets blow soft
Who the hell cares
Lets screw up some dots

I'll get in key while you play the head
you take a break now
I'll play instead
Lets play together
Lets heat the air...

We'll twist on the camber
We'll blow up some E.S.P.
Tap tap tappin our feet
Tap tap tappin
Tap tap tappin the beat
Yeah just tappin
tappin...

Said hey mister man
down on the street
Yeah I said you
Hey you mister jazz man still tappin your feet

Does it ever get lonely out there

17

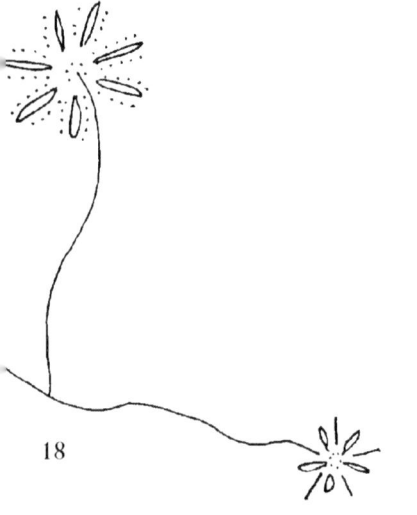

Once upon a time

We were all post war babies
infants of The Floyd
Pink with our tarnished innocence
And it was a pretty place once
when we lived in our blue kaleidoscope dreams
behaving like hoodlums in paradise
We were the villains of peace
The gangsters of the old millennium
We wrapped ourselves around our musk scented women
as we slept on the esplanades inside our castles in the air
and woke to the sound of the banshees screaming into the mere
running toward the Shangri-la we danced with our doppelgangers till dawn
and beside The Moon and Sixpence we had nothing
Nothing in our pockets our hearts raw laid bare
But life
Life
was bright as a new penny

The view from the window

No I don't want to sell out to mediocrity
to an oh too comfortable central heated
limp at the edges watery conversational
luke warm cocoa mortgage type of existence
of second best and it's alright maybe not what
I may have dreamed of kind of life
With suppers on my lap and the TV up so loud
drowning out the raging hunger within my heart
surrounded by books of yearning pages of
magic and mystery with the promise of
strange far off places never once visited
and CDs stacked full of songs of melancholic
hope and glory of opportunities
long past and missed

The view from the window as each spring
passes the wisteria chokes the rusted window
frames of the old slaughterhouse
where the blossom falls like broken hearts
bleeding across the benches of where lovers
once sat
Nature's epitaph for love lost and I have lost
count of how many times I've called your name
beneath whispers under my breath in public
places too gutless to scream it through the
streets for fear of being classed
Not Normal
But if this is the alternative I fear that
I have already made my choice
For I live here by the old slaughterhouse
and the view from the window as each spring
passes
I watch the wisteria choking the rusted window
frames as the blossom falls like broken hearts
bleeding across the benches of where
we as lovers once sat
Nature's epitaph for love lost
No
I took my chances

a lonely messiah

i sit in a room facing walls that are strange to me
covering my eyes as one might with a blanket or sheet when one wakes to morning
and looking through the thin linen my skin breathing
as perhaps an ankle swollen might feel in a china white bowl of cool scented water
shivering as one would rain sodden from the mood of winter
and smelling the bonfires on my sleeve
tasting the salt on my tongue as if caught in a clasp of wind by some promenade tide
tears swallowed like oysters repeated at the back of my throat as they rippled through my body reminded me of one tender autumn
sleeping at the edges along the kerbs of drives and avenues lay in their crowded comas the spirits of october sacrificing themselves to november
waiting for the street sweepers to sweep as they do

i remembered that night
when the pillars of the ice palace melted
when loneliness was arrested and the
rattle of handcuffs inaudible if only for a moment
and i felt that i wish i had never in my life
been intimate with anyone before
as you had explained
as if a child might seeing snow for the
first time or something like that and i
only wish
that i could have said the same

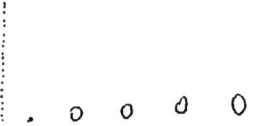

My urban lover

I can't imagine a life without you
remember when you told me that
dewdrops are nature's diamonds
not in so many words but during those
moody plasticine days when we locked
time away in a prism
and hung it between the lattice windows
stretching the sunlight far longer than it
wanted to be
we leaned over the landings and flew over
the jetties pretending to be Pegasus and
ransacked every lighthouse and attic room
along the way just for the pure devilment of it
and when we came upon jukebox dreams
and fire escape love and found it to be
crammed up full of broken hearts
we left them alone to weep into the
tarmac in private

But sometimes you would run up to me in your cotton field
dresses and kiss me
and your eyes were aflame with the colour of England
mulled wine and chestnut fires
and you sucked my tongue yes and I sucked your tongue with
a relentless reckless passion and you loved kissing my scars
as we got drunk on liqueur chocolates and drowned in liquid
liquorice while we took forbidden steps
jumping over the catseyes in the rain like tube trains kissing
in a mist and I chased you
chased you through the mewses and the glebes and you ran
from me but I was chasing the butterfly in your heart and
scuffling with the tragic dreams in my head
and all the things we would never have the time to do
even if we had the rest of our lives
but I like the person I have become with you
I like the person I am with you

Walk Talk Eat

walk WITH ME talk WITH ME eat WITH ME drink WITH ME
sing WITH ME song WITH ME run WITH ME dance WITH ME
laugh WITH ME cry WITH ME wash WITH ME dress WITH ME
jazz WITH ME blues WITH ME booze WITH ME groove WITH
ME shake WITH ME sweat WITH ME sleep WITH ME sex
WITH ME fuck WITH ME love WITH ME touch WITH ME ache
WITH ME look WITH ME fight WITH ME scream WITH ME
shout WITH ME push WITH ME pull WITH ME flip WITH ME
twist WITH ME hurt WITH ME grow WITH ME climb WITH
ME live WITH ME child WITH ME joy WITH ME sad WITH
ME joy WITH ME give TO ME take FROM ME give TO ME
give TO ME give TO ME take FROM ME take FROM ME try
WITH ME swim WITH ME drown WITH ME starve WITH ME
feast WITH ME flirt WITH ME learn WITH ME drift WITH
ME dream WITH ME age WITH ME die WITH ME
MARRY ME

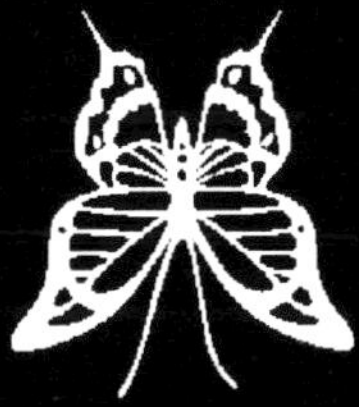

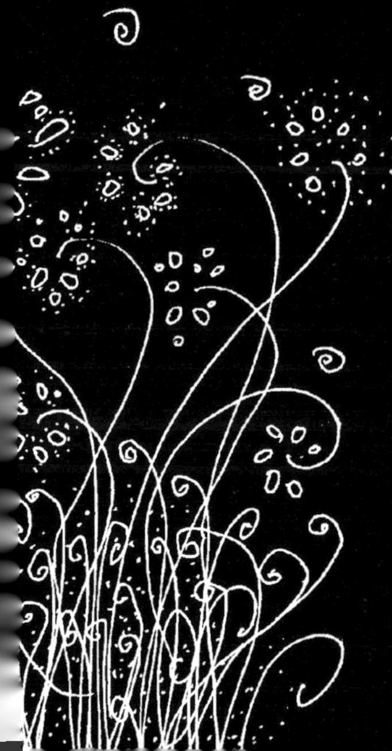

Ten rows back

Footsteps   flirted with echoes
Incense
Smoke smeared air
Gothic
Bell blazing spires sang out scattering paper blue petals
fluttering to bloom

The click of this rainbow projector behind my eyes
slowly faltered from low spark
Frame by frame
Still by still
Our song unsung
Flickered like a lantern within a lantern

Timelessness shared
Like wind blown silken threads lost upon a balcony of dreams
almost beckoned
as silence suspended itself for a moment

Swollen within tears
Shaded behind glass
Hanging on the very whisper of priest's words
yet to be spoken

Sitting ten rows back

I wanted to say something

&&&:::

Theodore & Grace

The roses are grey not red
not wine coloured ||: or whisky shaped
Their lifelessness full of the threat of joy
a precarious Theodore angry for a summer

The roses are grey not red
not scent-full like a violent crème de menthe
raped across a stale bartop
The psychotherapist of so many tales
another rubber Brando fat gagged
obese with tears fallen from grace

Roses are red
violence is not always black-blue
or nil by mouth
Co-habitating with mediocrity
that constant shapelessness
it pierces the child in your heart
A world where the roses are grey
not wine coloured :||

Bastards

I live in a desert
There are no passion trees there anymore
Not since
There are all sorts of other types of trees
bearing fruits of one kind or another
But it's the passion trees I miss most

They're great to climb
Swing and weave between the branches
Should you reach the top
Bolts of gold edged with silver
surge through your body till you shake
It's beautiful to climb the passion tree

It's Red ~ Red ~ all of it

I look for them ~ the passion trees
Hiding behind a vast space
or just casually standing idly beside an old fence

They came and cut them all down
Bastards
Thousands of them
It only took them an hour

The thing about passion trees is
you can fell them with words
No need for axe or saw

I live in a desert
There are no passion trees there
Just scars hollows
Gold edged with silver turned to sand and white

I live in a desert
No passion trees there anymore

Father figure

I never really knew him
Well at least I don't think I did
He wasn't at all what I thought he might be like
Not the cool silent type like I had imagined
Not at all like that really
Not that I ever met him face to face or anything like that
Well not really
It wasn't like you could make an appointment with him to see him
He wasn't that sort of person
not the sort of person that would expect you to
It was just that that wasn't his way making appointments and all that kind of thing
Nothing so formal
He was casual
Polite
But direct
Youthful
Not false though
Not like some people you meet

They seem really nice to begin with and all
kind of pally but you kind of know it
doesn't add up to much
No he wasn't like that
In fact he wasn't very pally at all but he
didn't make you feel uncomfortable
or anything like that quite the reverse
Made me feel like I didn't have to explain
anything much
Like he knew what I was going to say
before I said it so I didn't
He was one of those sort of people who
made you feel very special
Like you really mattered
Like you really were part of something
It was like all the things that you believed
in the things you fought for
the things or people you cared for till you
thought your heart would bust
actually *counted* for something
and I don't mean just for yourself
He made you feel like the *whole world*
was listening
when you said something that was close
to your heart

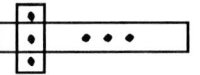

You know
Really private
But it was alright because they all
understood
He understood
And he didn't smile when he talked or
anything like that
well not with his mouth anyway
He was very serious really
almost solemn you might say
But not stern or stuffy
nothing like that
In fact for a moment
maybe even longer
I felt like I'd never not known him in a way
that's kind of hard to explain
and the last time we talked
he said something that really struck me
He was always doing that
More than once he'd done that
Just when I was playing Barber's Adagio
Or I remember once
just as I was catching the 86 (or I don't
know was it the 85)
or smoking a Number 6 or even both

No
I never really knew him
Well - not really
But he *knew* me
and the thing he said
that really struck me
It made me think
He said

He said
You're no accident

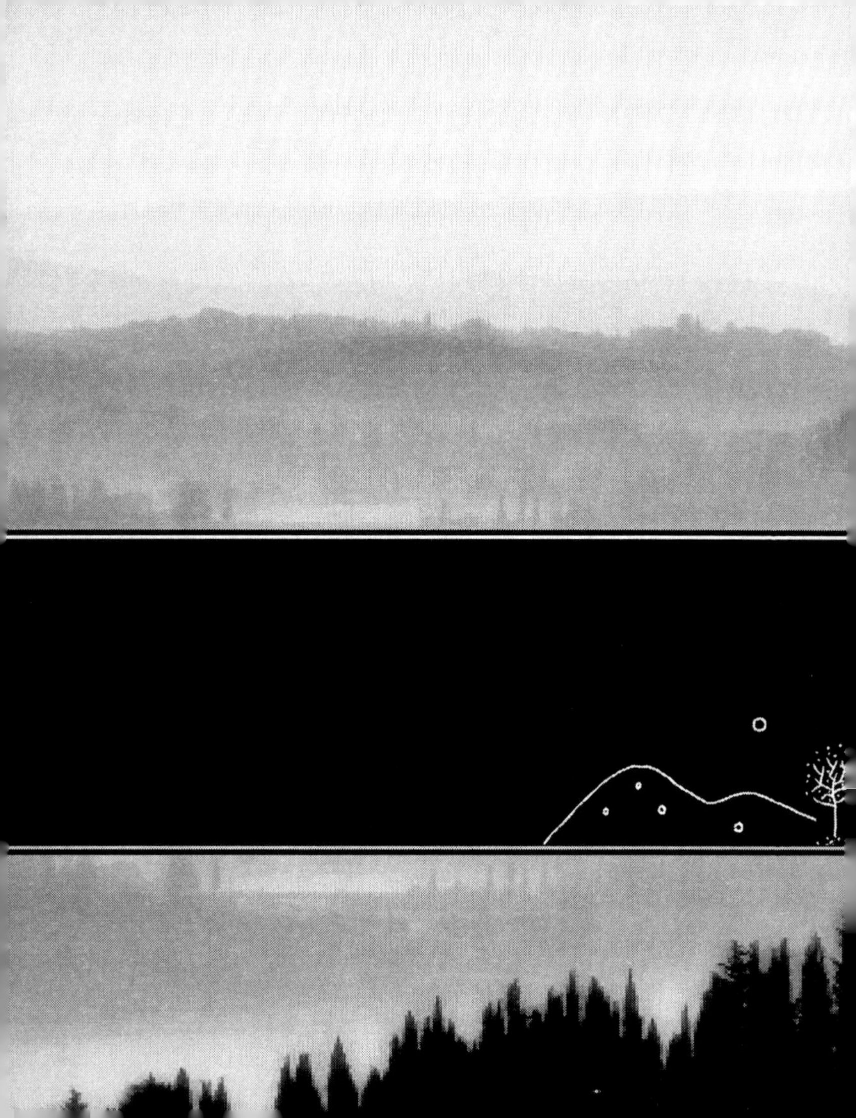

Box

Daniel put his head around my room door last night and said
if you had a box what would it be like and what would you keep in it
he said that when he did his English A level that's what they asked him
I didn't think anything of it at the time
but it got my brain rattling and I wondered what he would make of what I would tell him about my box
about what I would keep in it and what it might look like

spherical
like a cricket ball
made of heavy steel
covered in taut soft smooth
dark
red
crimson
leather
and you know where the stitches are the way they run round the centre in a narrow stripe
well it wouldn't have stitches there
it would have an ancient turquoise and black design like the early batiks of Indonesia
or like the old Egyptian wall paintings
and it would unscrew into two halves with a gold inner lip
and when you opened it
it would glow of amber and keep your face warm
and inside

inside it would have lots of tiny photographs in ornate miniature silver frames of all the people and places I loved most
so that when I was alone on a platform waiting for a train or sitting in an empty doctor's surgery
I could take them out of one half and look at them one by one placing them in the other
and when I had looked at them all I would screw the empty half back on
and every time it would create a different pattern around the centre where the stitches should be
and then when I put it back in my pocket it would bulge a bit and pull the shoulder of my jacket down a little making my collar look funny

or maybe it would be small but tall
oblong like
and making up the sides would be four paper thin stained glass windows each of different colours
all arched at the top and surrounded by apple twig frames
but the bottom panel would be transparent so you could see in from underneath
the lid would be kind of roof shaped
an apex of plain glass panes
pale shades of blue and green that fitted perfectly on top of the apple twig arches
and inside I would keep all my very special thoughts and feelings so I could take them out and think them or feel them whenever I wanted to

or it might be soft
a 50p shaped box
with yellow denim sides and purple dots and
a large round cork in the top
and it would be filled with infectious laughter
you know the kind you can't help but join in
with when you hear it
and I would open it under the table when my
posh and proper aunty was serving tea
and laugh until the tears streamed down my
cheeks

or maybe it would be shaped like a huge
treasure chest
you know the ones like the old pirates
used to use to smuggle rum and silks
from lands far across the seas
wooden with old brass studs
worn leather straps
buckles locks and keys
and not even I would know what was
inside it

but I don't think it would be like any of
these

if I had a box I would fill it full of sight and
give it to the people whose eyes couldn't
see

I'd fill it with cures for aids and cancer
and cures for all those other things that
can't be cured

I'd fill it full of food
decent food
tons of it
and send it to Somalia
I'd fill it full of tea and coffee and take it
round in cups to give to the miners or
the ambulancemen or the nurses or
anyone else who is threatened with
extinction or sentenced to live a cheap life

if it was made of bricks or stones I'd unstick
them all and put them back together by building
new houses where there had been earthquakes
winds and floods
and if it were made of timber I would chop it up
and build fires in the streets to keep people
warm who had nowhere to go at Christmas
time or any other time for that matter
to stop them from freezing to death in
temperatures below f-ing zero
and I'd keep building fires so that people took
notice and made empty office blocks places
people could live in

or maybe my box would be a massive aquarium
as big as the Empire State
full of plants and rocks
where I'd put all the dolphins and whales that
keep getting used for target practice
so that they could swim around freely
and I would build a couple of
elevators that ran up the sides
and I would go up and down all day
just watching them

or I might just turn it into thousands of
comfortable kennels

where all the cats and dogs that were
unwanted birthday presents could live until
Noah came to fetch them

I'd fill it full of time and give it to people who
didn't have any for each other anymore

I think I would fill it with semi permanent blue
paint that lasted for a year
so that when I saw someone who was being
cruel to somebody else just because they are
a different colour
I'd spray them from head to toe and after the
year had gone by
I would ask them what it was like to be blue
living in a society that's black and white

I'd fill it full of shit
making sure that it was big enough to get a
shovel in
and feed it to the arseholes who
abuse human rights and everything that
stands for humanity and equality

I'd gather every gun
sword and weapon that had ever been made
put them in a box and bury it
where no-one could ever find it
and I'd put all the people who want to go on
killing each other in another one
so far away from anything or anybody
so that you couldn't hear them squabbling
and I'd lock it up and throw away the key

I'd turn my box into lots of homes
where parents who couldn't have children
could meet children who didn't have parents

I'd put a big cross on top of it along with all
the symbols of the world's religions and a
huge sign that says
'All People Are Welcome Here'
so that people didn't have to fight over the
same God
and so that people could learn to understand
that we pray in different ways

I would take my box everywhere I went and I
would fill it with the most beautiful flowers
and on Saturday nights I would walk the
streets of every red light area in every town
and give a flower to every prostitute I could
find

I'd keep my matches in it to light my
cigarettes

I'd keep a bloody great alarm clock in it so I
could get up in the morning
I'd pee in it when I'd been shopping
in town and there wasn't a loo to be found
I'd stuff it full of Cadbury's Creme Eggs and
only give them to my best friends

I'd fill it up with foam
jump into it
and foam people out
and if it were a crate
I'd hide in it and sit on the dock waiting for a
crane to swoop down on me
pick me up and load me onto a ship
with an unknown destination

or maybe I'd fill it to the brim with
brilliant dazzling sunlight
and one dark starless night I'd creep into the
park and let it out

or I might just fill it with tender love songs
or my favourite days
which I didn't want to let drift into the past

maybe I'd crawl into it and having packed
it full of cotton wool
I'd roll up like a ball pulling the lid down tight
so the world couldn't get me

maybe I'd fill it with poems I wanted
no-one to read

but to tell the truth if I had a box
I think my box would look a little like me
and I would keep lots of things in it
things that you can't always see

and the only one who would really know
what was in it
right down in the deepest furthermost corner
of it would be me

if you had a box
what do you think it would look like
what would you keep in it

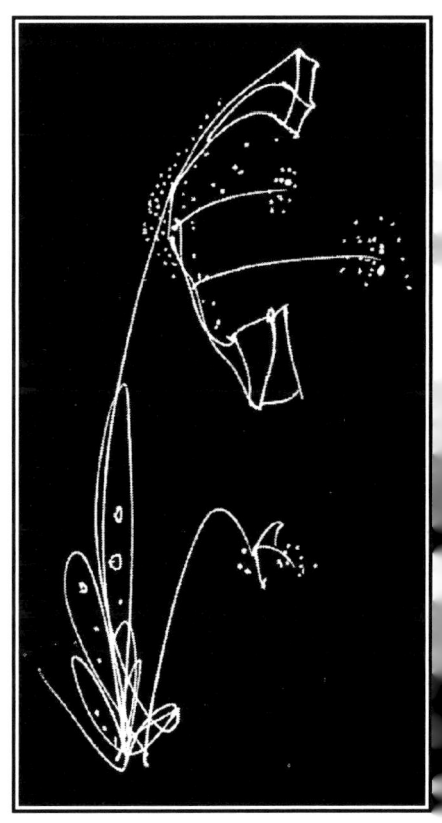

colour of morning

colour of morning

*..the truest love could never be the thief of another's heart,
only the gift of one's own*